RYNE SANDBERG

JOHNNY EVERS

SAMMY SOSA

HACK WILSON

ALBERT SPALDING

MARK GRACE

FRANK CHANCE

RICK SUTCLIFFE

ERNIE BANKS

KERRY WOOD

GABBY HARTNETT

ANDRE DAWSON

THE HISTORY OF THE

CHICAGO
CUBS

AARON FRISCH

CREATIVE EDUCATION

Published by Creative Education, 123 South Broad Street, Mankato, MN 56001

Creative Education is an imprint of The Creative Company.

Designed by Rita Marshall.

Photographs by AllSport (Jonathan Daniel, Jamie Squire), Associated Press/Wide World Photos,

Icon Sports Media (John Biever), National Baseball Library, SportsChrome (Jonathan Kirn,

Rob Tringali Jr., TimePix (John Dominis)

Library of Congress Cataloging-in-Publication Data

Frisch, Aaron. The history of the Chicago Cubs / by Aaron Frisch.

p. cm. — (Baseball)   ISBN 1-58341-203-4

Summary: Highlights the key personalities and memorable games in the history of the

team that began major league play in 1876 under the name White Stockings.

1. Chicago Cubs (Baseball team)—History—

Juvenile literature. [1. Chicago Cubs (Baseball team)—History.

2. Baseball—History.] I. Title. II. Baseball (Mankato, Minn.).

GV875.C58 F75 2002   796.357'64'0977311—dc21   2001047854

9 8 7 6 5 4 3

WITH A

Illinois, is the biggest and most influential city in the Midwest.

The city has been known by several nicknames over the years. It is

sometimes called the "City of Broad Shoulders," a reference to the

hardworking, industrious reputation of its citizens. Chicago is also **5**

known as the "Windy City" because of the ever-present breeze that

blows off of Lake Michigan.

Those winds add to the unique atmosphere of Wrigley Field, a

baseball stadium that is a Chicago landmark. That stadium, known

for its ivy-covered outfield wall and cozy dimensions, has been

home to a National League (NL) baseball team called the Cubs

since the 1920s. Although the Cubs, one of the NL's charter

ALBERT SPALDING

members way back in 1876, have not been the game's most successful franchise, they have always been among the most beloved.

{THE TURN-OF-THE-CENTURY CUBS} The Cubs were founded by William A. Hulbert in the early 1870s and were originally known as the White Stockings. The team suffered one losing season after another in its early years, and mounting problems throughout professional baseball—including gambling scandals and generally poor play—threatened to destroy the game itself.

Facing these problems, Hulbert decided to take action. He met with owners of other pro teams in 1876 and talked them into forming a new league called the National League. The owners put together rules for league play and player conduct. Hulbert then brought in several outstanding players, including pitcher Albert Spalding, to make sure his team would be competitive.

MARK GRACE

Doubling as manager and first baseman, Cap Anson led Chicago for 18 seasons.

CAP ANSON

With Spalding leading the way, the White Stockings emerged as a powerhouse. The star pitcher—who was also the team's manager—was practically the entire team at times, racking up an astounding 47 wins in 1876. The White Stockings finished with a 52–14 record and captured the very first NL pennant.

In **1886**, outfielder King Kelly batted .388 and stole 53 bases to help Chicago win the pennant.

A few years later, Spalding retired and founded a successful sporting goods company. Replacing him as Chicago's manager was Adrian "Cap" Anson. Anson kept the White Stockings on top, leading them to five NL pennants between 1880 and 1886. "Cap Anson was a baseball pioneer," noted an early sportswriter. "He was one of the first to use coaching signals, the hit-and-run, a pitching rotation, and spring training. He was also a mean-spirited guy who…demanded very strict behavior. His players often hated him, but he helped them become winners."

9

KING KELLY

Built in **1914**, Wrigley Field is the game's second-oldest ballpark (after Fenway Park).

WRIGLEY FIELD

In the early 1900s, the White Stockings got another new manager and a new name. The new manager was Frank Chance,

who also played first base when he took the helm in 1906. For years, the club had been known as the Cubs to some fans, and as the Colts or Nationals to others. (During that era it was common for teams to go by several different names at once.) In 1907, the team officially became the Cubs, a reference to its youthful lineup.

In Chance's first season as manager, Chicago rolled to a stunning 116–36 record. Powering the team that year were two great pitchers: Ed Reulbach and Mordecai "Three-Finger" Brown (who had lost the use of two digits in a childhood farming accident). The two hurlers were a devastating combination, but they could not lead the White Stockings past their crosstown rivals—the American League champion Chicago White Sox—in the 1906 World Series.

MORDECAI BROWN

The next season, the Cubs won their first world championship,

easily beating the Detroit Tigers in the World Series. In 1908,

second baseman Johnny Evers and shortstop Joe Tinker sparked

Chicago as the Cubs topped the Tigers again in the World Series.

Faithful Cubs fans were ecstatic, not knowing how long their wait

would be for another world championship.

{GABBY BRINGS THE CUBBIES BACK} The Cubs played

erratic baseball over the next 20 years. They won a couple more

pennants but suffered a number of poor seasons as

well. The team bottomed out in 1925, sinking to an

NL-worst 68–86 mark. Fortunately, help soon arrived

in the form of two new stars: catcher Charles "Gabby"

Hartnett and center fielder Lewis "Hack" Wilson.

Chicago set a modern era (since **1900**) team record by scoring 26 runs in one game in **1922**.

14

Hartnett joined the Cubs in 1922. He was an excellent

defender and hitter, but he earned his nickname with his habit of

talking to opposing hitters at the plate. A team leader, Gabby

used his nonstop chatter to annoy opponents and motivate his

teammates. "He got the best out of you...," said Cubs pitcher

Charlie Root. "He was daring at all times and sure of himself. He

made a pitcher feel that way, too."

Wilson arrived in Chicago in 1926. He looked like George

ERIC YOUNG

Hackenschmidt, a famous wrestler of that era, so his teammates

began calling him "Hack." Wilson stood only 5-foot-6, but at a well-

muscled 200 pounds, he was extremely powerful. With his unusual

tomahawk swing, he regularly smashed screaming line drives over

the Wrigley Field fences. In 1930, Wilson hit 56 home runs and

drove in 191 runs—both league records that stood for decades.

The Cubs won NL pennants in 1929, 1932, 1935, and 1938 but came up short in the World Series every year. One of the most memorable games in Cubs history took place during the 1938 season. Late that year, the Cubs trailed the Pittsburgh Pirates by half a game in the NL standings. The two teams squared off at Wrigley Field, and the score was tied 5–5 going into the ninth inning. But there was a problem: there were no lights at Wrigley Field and it was getting dark. The umpires announced that the game would be called if neither team scored in the ninth.

The Cubs retired three straight Pittsburgh batters, but the first two Chicago batters made outs as well. Then Hartnett stepped to the plate. The darkness made it almost impossible to see, and Hartnett took two quick strikes. When the third pitch came whizzing toward the plate, Gabby swung where he thought the ball might be, and he

Stout slugger Hack Wilson was a four-time NL home run champion in the **1920s** and '**30s**.

HACK WILSON

The Cubs'
history spans
more than
125 years
and includes
nearly 1,700
players.

connected. A roar went up as the ball sailed through the dark sky

into the left-field stands. Hartnett's famous shot, known as the

Hall of Fame
shortstop
Ernie Banks
set an NL
record by
swatting five
grand slams
in **1955**.
"homer in the gloamin' [darkness]," helped make the

Cubs NL champs once again.

{THE GREAT "MR. CUB"} The Cubs won

another pennant in 1945 but then steadily declined

for the next 20 years. Some great players starred in

20 Chicago during the 1950s and '60s but never knew the thrill of

winning a championship. Among those "ringless" stars were

outfielder Billy Williams, hard-hitting third baseman Ron Santo,

shortstop Don Kessinger, and pitchers Moe Drabowsky, Ken

Holtzman, and Fergie Jenkins.

But perhaps the Cubs player who most deserved a World

Series ring was the man known as "Mr. Cub": shortstop Ernie Banks.

In 19 seasons in Chicago, Banks won the adoration of Cubs fans

ERNIE BANKS

with his warm smile, mighty swing, and sure glove. Even though the

Cubs were a losing team for most of his career, Banks's enthusiasm

never waned. Rain or shine, whenever someone would ask Banks

about the weather, he would invariably reply, "It's a beautiful day

for baseball. Let's play two [a doubleheader]!"

At 6-foot-1 and 180 pounds, Banks didn't look like a slugger.

But he had steely arms and strong wrists that allowed him to generate amazing power. Banks crushed 47 and 45 home runs in 1958 and 1959, respectively, and was named the NL's Most Valuable Player (MVP) each season. Over the course of his remarkable career, Banks played in 14 All-Star Games and clouted 512 home runs—accomplishments that made him the first Cubs player to have his number (14) retired.

All-Star pitcher Fergie Jenkins led the Cubs with 20 or more wins a season from **1967** to **1972**.

After Banks retired in 1971, the Cubs' struggles continued. By then, the team played in the NL Eastern Division (the league was split into two divisions in 1969), and the Pittsburgh Pirates and Philadelphia Phillies dominated the division throughout the 1970s. Pitcher Bruce Sutter and outfielder Dave Kingman gave Chicago fans some highlights during those years, but by 1980, the Cubs had missed the playoffs for 35 straight seasons.

FERGIE JENKINS

Like Ernie
Banks, Sammy
Sosa's enthu-
siasm and
booming bat
made him a
fan favorite.

SAMMY SOSA

{SANDBERG, GRACE, AND A POSTSEASON TASTE} The

Cubs finally broke their postseason drought in 1984 by winning the

NL East title. Leading the way that season was veteran

pitcher Rick Sutcliffe. With his burly 6-foot-5 frame,

red beard, and intimidating pitching style, Sutcliffe

was known as the "Red Baron." The big right-hander

went 16–1 and won the Cy Young Award as the

NL's best pitcher.

Versatile star Ryne Sandberg stole 54 bases in **1985**, the most by a Cubs player in 79 years.

Also enjoying a career season in 1984 was a young second

baseman named Ryne Sandberg. That year, Sandberg batted .314,

stole 32 bases, and performed nearly flawlessly in the field to walk

away with the NL MVP award. Radio and television announcer

Harry Caray, the legendary voice of the Cubs, summed up Sandberg's

versatile talents best: "I've been calling big-league games for 40 years,

and I can't remember anybody capturing the imaginations of the fans

RYNE SANDBERG

quite like this kid."

Throughout the 1980s, the Cubs continued adding talented

players in an attempt to build a champion. In 1987, the team signed

veteran outfielder Andre "the Hawk" Dawson. Although he was no

longer the swift and agile fielder he once was, Dawson could still

hit. In his first season in Chicago, he crushed 49 home runs and racked up 137 RBI—numbers that earned him NL MVP honors.

By 1989, the Cubs' lineup also included shortstop Shawon

Dunston, a defensive marvel, and outfielder Jerome

Walton. Chicago won its division again that season,

and a new star emerged in the playoffs: first baseman

Mark Grace. Against the San Francisco Giants in the

NL Championship Series, Grace batted at a .647 clip

and drove in eight runs. Unfortunately, the Cubs once again fell

short of the World Series.

Dawson left town in 1992, but a new slugger took his place in

right field: Sammy Sosa. A native of the Dominican Republic, Sosa

combined the uplifting cheerfulness of Ernie Banks with the raw

power of Hack Wilson. "Sosa's a classic slugger," admired Giants

manager Dusty Baker. "Every time up, he might take one deep."

Throughout all of the team's personnel changes, there was

ANDRE DAWSON

always one constant in Chicago—Ryne Sandberg. But the Cubs

continued to struggle in the mid-1990s, and Sandberg brought his

A renowned
fireballer,
Cubs reliever
Randy Myers
nailed down
a league-
leading 38
saves in **1995**.

stellar career to a close in 1997. "I've worn this

uniform a long time, and I'm proud of all I've

accomplished as a Cub," he said. "But I wish I could

have brought the fans here a World Series."

{SLAMMIN' SAMMY SETS THE PACE} The

Cubs didn't bring Chicago fans a World Series in 1998 either, but

there was plenty of excitement at Wrigley Field that season. One

reason was the play of flamethrowing rookie pitcher Kerry Wood,

who tied a major-league record by striking out 20 batters in one

game against Houston early in the season. "He's 20 years old," Mark

Grace marveled. "He doesn't even know how good he is."

Wood was great, but the player who really kept fans riveted

in 1998 was Sosa. That season, Sosa and St. Louis slugger Mark

RANDY MYERS

McGwire matched each other home run for home run in a race to break the major-league record of 61 homers in a season. Both players eclipsed the record late in the season, with McGwire swatting 70 home runs and Sosa finishing with 66.

Even though he didn't set the new home run record, Sosa did win the NL MVP award with a league-best 158 RBI. Perhaps more importantly, he led the Cubs to a 90–73 record and a wild-card berth in the playoffs. Chicago fell to Atlanta in the playoffs, but the loss took nothing away from what was truly a magical season.

Unfortunately, Wood struggled with an elbow injury in the seasons that followed, and the Cubs faded from the playoff picture. Shortstop Jeff Blauser, second baseman Eric Young, pitcher Jon Lieber, and closer Tom Gordon gave their all, but the Cubs remained in the middle of the standings. Through it all, though,

Right fielder Henry Rodriguez did his best to boost Chicago in **1999**, slamming 26 homers.

HENRY RODRIGUEZ

Young start-
ing pitcher
Kerry Wood
was known
for his 100-
miles-per-hour
fastball.

KERRY WOOD

Closer Tom "Flash" Gordon had a fine **2001** season, ending the year with 27 saves.

TOM GORDON

Sosa remained a much-needed bright spot. From 1998 to 2001,

he slammed a total of 243 home runs, becoming the first player in

major-league history to hit 60 or more homers in

three seasons.

By 2002, it had been 57 years since the Chicago Cubs

had appeared in a World Series and 94 years since

they had won a world championship. Yet despite the

long drought, Cubs fans pack the bleachers at Wrigley Field year

after year. As a new century unfolds, the Cubs hope that the winds

that blow through Chicago are soon winds of change for the better.

FRED McGRIFF